Truth and Love

in a sexually

disordered world

Truth and Love

in a sexually

disordered world

Editor: David Searle

Published for

RUTHERFORD HOUSE

by

paternoster
publishing

Published 1997 by Paternoster Publishing, P.O. Box 300,
Carlisle, Cumbria, CA3 0QS UK, and Rutherford House,
17 Claremont Park, Edinburgh EH6 7PJ, Scotland

02   01 00 99 98 97   7 6 5 4 3 2 1

British Library Cataloguing in Publication Data

A catalogue record for this book is available from
the British Library

ISBN 0-946068-67-4

Typeset by Rutherford House, Edinburgh
and printed in the UK by
Mackays of Chatham PLC, Kent

PREFACE

This little book is a collection of papers that have been given by different people in different places to different audiences at different times. Though they may as a consequence lack some cohesion, they have the sharpness and directness of their original presentation.

The first two chapters attempt to offer in-depth expositions of sexuality in two key sections of Scripture, and Geoffrey Grogan's treatment of Romans 1 also involves a critique of some contemporary attempts to offer alternative interpretations of the apostle Paul's attitude towards homosexuality. Both these papers were first prepared in 1994 as a submission from Rutherford House to the Church of Scotland's *ad hoc* committee on Sexuality.

David's Wright's chapter on issues raised by the homosexuality debate first appeared as an editorial in the Spring 1995 issue of *The Rutherford Journal of Church & Ministry* (Vol.2.1). William Still's contribution was originally a paper delivered to the Crieff Conference in 1992. Chapter 5 is taken from the Reports to the General Assembly of the Church of Scotland, 1995, and is used by kind permission of the Assembly Clerk.

The chapter on Singleness is adapted and abbreviated from an address given at Carberry in November 1995 to a conference convened for single people of both sexes. Chapter 7 was an address given to Grace Church, Greenwich, Connecticut, in December 1995.

Several of the chapters may be used as the basis for a series of group Bible Studies. I have refrained from including suggested questions for discussion, though I do believe that much of the material offers evangelical comment on Scripture passages which need to be studied afresh in the light of contemporary attitudes. The Church is always at her best when she rediscovers the relevance of Scripture and so reaffirms her fidelity to the Word of God.

It is the editor's and contributors' hope and prayer that this diverse collection will be of some value in stimulating discussion and enabling Christians today to see and understand more clearly the crucial issues involved in the current sexuality debate.

David C Searle,
Rutherford House, Edinburgh
September 1996

Contents

INTRODUCTION

After centuries of neglecting the problems that arise from our human sexuality in the vain hope that these problems will somehow go away if we ignore them, it is surely right and proper that the Church today should be urgently addressing them. However, it is clearly important that the method we adopt must be both appropriate and valid. Otherwise, any conclusions will be flawed, and the problems on which we have worked to throw light will be as clouded as they have been in the past.

There are two possible approaches to problems associated with our human sexuality. One way of proceeding might be to begin with an investigation of what people who are affected by such problems themselves feel and think. From there, the expertise of those who have sought to work with them in a supportive role could be tapped. In this way, up to date thinking would become available for those seeking to come to terms with sexual problems.

But grave doubts must hang over this method of working. The opinions of any section of contemporary society are bound to be as shifting as the pattern left on the sand by the ebbing tide. Truth itself becomes relative, and accommodates itself to the current vogue in any culture's thinking. An alternative approach must therefore be sought.

Christians believe, and those ordained to the Ministry of Word and Sacraments in our Church avow, that Scripture is the final source of authority in all matters of faith and conduct. Our method, therefore, must be to seek to assess as accurately and fairly as it is possible to do, what the Bible says on all problems which arise from our human sexuality. This will at least give us a starting point from which to work, and a basis for our endeavours to provide pastoral love and care, and full acceptance into the Church's fellowship of those who in the past may have felt excluded.

When we begin with Scripture, we at once discover that every living person has departed in thought and motive from the will of God in sexual behaviour, and since none is righteous in this area of living, there is no room for censorious attitudes. Dr Merville Vincent (quoted in *Issues facing Christians Today*, p. 302 by John W. R. Stott) says: 'In God's view I suspect we are all sexual deviants. I doubt if there is anyone who has not had a lustful thought that deviated from God's perfect ideal of sexuality'.

To uphold the standards of sexuality given in the Bible could be costly for the Church in her relationship to today's society. For standards are changing so rapidly that many of the younger generation no longer are aware that Christians believe God has provided clear standards for our sexuality. But unless the Church is to be influenced by society, instead of herself acting as salt and light in society, we Christians must not shrink from such distinctiveness, nor from the possible adverse response which may result. The light must be put on its stand; the city must continue to be seen standing high on the hill.

There is one obvious difference between starting with the way things are at present—how people think and behave—and starting with the Bible. The Bible starts with, and assumes throughout, heterosexuality, not with sexuality in a non-specific sense; whereas it is common today for discussion to begin with an indeterminate sexuality and only then to consider its different expressions. The Bible knows nothing of a floating sexual identity which may issue in a range of different sexual actions. Its basis throughout is unambiguously heterosexual—man and woman created sexually for each other. While Christians must always be sensitive to what is happening in society, it is crucial that we do not adopt a starting point which in this case would effectively silence the Bible's main voice and message on the issue.

In the following pages, various aspects of sexuality are dealt with. But whether the treatment is expository (as in chapters 1 and 7) or apologetic (as in chapters 2 and 3) or pastoral (as in chapters 4, 5 and 6), the starting point is always scripture. For our firm conviction is that God has spoken fully and finally in and through his Son, Jesus Christ. Using scripture as the starting point, each contributor seeks to show the relevance for today of orthodox Christian morality. How successful that endeavour has been will be measured by the usefulness of this book.

ONE

SEXUALITY IN GENESIS 1 AND 2

David C Searle

As we approach the subject of sexuality, we are aware of two extreme attitudes common today in any discussion of it.

First, there is the Victorian reluctance to speak candidly at all about sexuality: this was a subject that was taboo. Many today accuse the Victorians of hypocrisy and allege that beneath the cloak of silence were concealed repression and even cruelty. (Though there is undoubtedly truth in this charge, one has to remember that many Victorian homes were happy and balanced, the women there honoured, fulfilled and given worthy status).

Second, there is the opposite extreme of complete openness. The brilliant writer, D. H. Lawrence, breached the 19th century dam of secrecy, but the result has been that readiness to speak more openly about sexuality has led to a deluge of shameless exploitation. We are now invaded by an eroticism—almost a deification of sex—which has run out of control.

When we turn to the Biblical treatment of sexuality, we find a careful balance between these two extremes. While sexuality is spoken of with candour and honesty, it is nevertheless seen as a sacred gift of God not to be regarded with careless familiarity. In Genesis chs 1 and 2, we find neither Victorian prudery nor our modern shameless obsession with sex. Rather, sexuality is dealt with in language which is both beautiful and disciplined. However, the Church today often fails to reflect this Biblical balance and unfortunately the old Victorian attitudes are at times still reflected among many Christians.

Researching pre-biblical writings on this same subject is like wandering across the moors looking for water: there are plenty of pools, but they are all muddied or stagnant; until one suddenly comes upon a pool, unlike the rest, where the water is clean and uncontaminated. That pool is the Genesis treatment of sexuality. The pool is so clear that one's reflection can easily be seen in its pure waters.

But the Genesis tablets are unique in another way. They lay the basis for the Bible's whole thinking and teaching on this subject of sexuality. When Luther wrote that the early chapters of Genesis were foundational for all Biblical theology, sexuality was certainly included.

The likeness of man and woman

> Genesis 1:26f.: *Then God said, 'Let us make man in our image, in our likeness'...So God created man in his own image...male and female he created them.*

Twice over, the word *man* is used in a common sense of both male and female. We might even (as the New R.S.V. has done) translate *man* here by 'humankind'. This common meaning of the noun *man* is rapidly being lost, and many have assumed that there is a built-in male bias here.

Not so; the use of the noun *man* for both *male and female* is emphasising their **likeness**. It is laying down the principle that the man and the woman stand side by side as equals, distinct and apart from everything else God has made (...*let them rule over the fish of the sea and the birds of the air, over the livestock, over all the earth, and over all the creatures that move along the ground*...1:26b), with their very being as living souls (2:7 AV) the great common aspect of their existence. They are created standing side by side as equals.

The detail about the *rib* (2:21f.) teaches the same principle. There are at least three possible understandings *of tsela* (the rib). (i) It can be translated as 'side' (so NIV margin). This meaning underlines the 'side by sideness' of the man and the woman. We have in English a similar saying in the phrase, 'my other half'. (ii) A second meaning comes from Arabic where it means 'my closest friend' in the sense of one

who is at my very side and without whom I cannot do.
(iii) A third possible meaning comes from Sumerian
where it means 'life'. In 3:20, we are told that Adam
calls his wife 'Eve', meaning 'life'. Probably the best
translation is (i), that is, 'side'. The force of the idea of
the woman coming from the man's side is that they
make a perfect pair in their side-by-sideness. It is emphasising their likeness.

There is yet another aspect of the pair's likeness: it
comes first in their joint relationship to God as created
in his likeness. God created them in his image, first and
foremost, an equal pair, a pair of equals. If they are
honest, men have to make the confession that equality
has often been violated down the ages. Repeatedly, the
balance has been lost. We should note at this point two
distortions in thinking about sexuality which have come
to us through men's transgression against women's
equality.

The first is the unbiblical macho image of the man,
which is both foolish and arrogant. The Psalms tell us
plainly that God takes no pleasure in that kind of male
image (Ps. 147:10). Experience teaches us that men
acting out the macho image make bad husbands and
worse lovers. Women prefer men to be thoughtful, considerate, gentle and loving. The macho male distortion
roughly sets to one side the woman's equality with the
man.

The second distortion arising from this neglect of
the equality between the sexes is the false concept of

the Eternal Femininity on the one hand, and the reading of 'maleness' into God's nature on the other hand. The error of the concept of Eternal Femininity is that it introduces sexuality into the Godhead; likewise, it is a misunderstanding of Deity to read maleness into the fatherhood of God. Genesis 1:26f. is not saying that God made the male in his own image and likeness. *Man* made in the image of God, (that is, *male and female* created in the divine image), is stressing that in the likeness of the man and the woman to each other they are made in God's image and likeness. In other words, an important aspect of the image of God in humankind is the fundamental likeness of male and female to each other. If we make God either male or female, we drive a horse and carriage through that likeness, and embark on the foolish and vain endeavour to build a relationship with God on the basis of sexuality and male-female differentiation.

Reproduction, as we know it, requires both male and female. But God creates; he does not reproduce. Though Scripture thinks anthropomorphically about God, using both paternal and maternal concepts (*eg*, Luke 15:11ff. and Matt. 23:37), it is misleading and inaccurate to ascribe sexuality to God.

The difference between man and woman

In Genesis 1, God is represented as reviewing what he has done six times over and seeing that it is good. But in 2:18 there is a significant statement of something

that is not good, and this means there is something still
to be done:

> *The Lord God said, 'It is not good for the man to*
> *be alone. I will make a helper suitable for him'.*

And so came the woman, equal to the man, but yet
different to him. That is the principle being established
here. Male and female are not the same. They are essentially different, and the woman's femininity per-
meates her being (though her equality must not be sac-
rificed to that femininity).

There is a strong modern belief that, granted certain
necessary anatomical and physiological differences between the sexes, men and women are essentially the
same. Any differences which develop during childhood
are only the result of environmental conditioning. But
Genesis 2 is teaching there is an intended difference
between the sexes.

> *'I will make a helper suitable for him'.* NRSV: *'I*
> *will make him a helper as his partner'.*

The word *helper* speaks of co-operation, not rivalry,
because it was complementarity that was God's will
for the man and woman. Some women have objected
to the word helper as being both derogatory and patronising. But this word is used only 21 times in the
O.T., and 15 of those occurrences describe God as our
Helper lifting up broken, defeated and helpless men,
setting them on their feet and encouraging and strengthening them (*e.g.* Ex. 18:4; Deut. 33:7, 26, 29; Ps. 20:2;
33:20 *etc.*). Viewed contextually, this word is surely a

most lofty and worthy description of the difference between the man and the woman, for it is elevating her to fulfil a divine function.

The word *suitable* (*partner*) literally means 'an over against one' in the sense of a 'counterpart'; *corresponding to* would be a good translation. It carries the meaning of complete complementarity.

> 'I take [*suitable*] in its general sense, as though it were said she is a kind of counterpart, for the woman is said to be *opposite to*, or *over against*, the man, because she responds to him' (Calvin, Comm. *in loc.*).

The woman is therefore to be a contrary one to the man in the sense of positively stimulating and provoking him to ever higher endeavour. The man is incomplete without the woman. He needs her partnership and she has a role to play which makes both of them complete as a team of two.

By extrapolation, the complementarity of the man and woman is carried over into non-physical relationships of everyday living. In work, community and church, men and women are incomplete without each other, whereas in a proper relationship they form an effective team.

The difference that is so clearly implied in the sexual relationship of the man to the woman is their 'face-to-faceness', for Eve was Adam's bride. Just as their side-by-sideness was expressed in their relationship to God as created in his image, so their face-to-faceness also expresses their relationship to God as created in his image. For God is not a solitary being. *God said, 'Let us make man in our image, in our likeness...'* (1:26).

The Prologue of John's Gospel expounds the God of the Genesis account of creation as a Being with relationships within himself. *The Word was with God and the Word was God...the One and Only, who came from the Father...God the One and Only, who is at the Father's side...*(John 1:1, 14, 18).

Therefore, it is in both our likeness to God, made in his image *male and female*, and in our difference to him, created by him as the work of his hands, that our relationship to God lies. Both **likeness** and **difference** are needed. The Biblical principle taught here is that it is only as the man and the woman face God that they can face each other in fullness of complementarity.

Is this not the error of modern extreme feminism, that it seeks to have male and female stand side by side, but not face to face? It encourages women to see men as rivals, instead of as partners. And so sexuality becomes misunderstood and distorted, for in rivalry there can never be complementarity, far less true unity. And the beautiful and glorious truth of the Genesis theology of sexuality is that male and female become one in their likeness and one in their difference, in their side-by-sideness, and in their face-to-faceness. *The man and his wife were both naked, and they felt no shame* (2:25).

It is here that we come up against the essence of sin

in any homosexual genital relationship. Whether a male–male, or a female–female, sexual relationship, it is bound to be based on likeness, but not on difference. So such a relationship is based not only on just a part of human sexuality, but on a seriously deficient relationship with God. For the relationship of humankind to God is, by creation, founded on both likeness and difference.

The order between man and woman

We come to the N.T. understanding of the theology contained in the order of creation, in that the man was made first, and then the woman. Paul takes this to mean that the man is the *head* of the woman (1Cor. 11:3; Eph. 5:23; 1Tim. 2:13).

> The head of every man is Christ, the head of woman is man, and the head of Christ is God (1Cor. 11:3).

It is axiomatic in Pauline theology that Christ is the Son of God, and as the Son, is co-equal with the Father. The name which is above every name, that he is Lord, implies his deity and equality with God. Nevertheless, Paul can also say that *the head of Christ is God.* So in some way, equality does not exclude headship on the one hand, nor submission to that headship on the other hand.

The Hebrew understanding of *the head* needs to be studied in detail (which is outwith the scope of this article on Genesis 1 & 2). But we can affirm that in

Hebrew thought 'thinking' and 'mind' were not thought of as within the head. Rather, the head was seen as the source of life. And since Adam was created first in Genesis 2, it is not difficult to see why Paul calls him *the head*.

God is called *the head of Christ*, since the Son is eternally begotten. God's headship of Christ speaks of the eternal generation of the Son, that is, the Son eternally derives life from the Father. The Son is head of the Church in that he is *first born* of the resurrection, and thus the prototype of the new creation. But since God raised him from the dead, God is still his source of life.

But the other side of the coin is undoubtedly the submission which is given by Christ to God as head, and which the woman is invited to give to the man as head. There can be no doubt that the reason for the common objections raised to such submission is given in Genesis 3:16c: *Your desire will be for your husband...* (*cf.* 4:7b:*...sin is crouching at your door; it desires to have you...*), and the meaning appears to be that the Fall has robbed the man-woman relationship of its perfect complementarity, and substituted in its place an uneasy rivalry.

But there is no such rivalry between Father and Son (Phil. 3:6ff....*Who, being in very nature God, did not consider equality with God something to be grasped, but made himself nothing etc.*), and therefore Christ's submission to his Father was an expression of perfect love for the Father, as was the Father's will for the Son.

Headship in the N.T. sense, therefore, can only work harmoniously when both man and woman are in Christ, and the submission of the woman (as an equal to an equal) is lovingly offered to the man as a gift from one who is both side by side, and face to face, with him. More, if the woman does not freely give that submission, then the 'order between man and woman' in Christ cannot happen. By the same token, unless the man, with Christ also as his role-model, does not love the woman with a sacrificial, self-denying, self-giving love (Eph. 5:25ff.), then neither can his headship be a harmonious constituent of the partnership.

Adam was formed first…(1Tim. 3:13). The underlying principle in the Hebrew mind of Paul is probably that of the responsibility the first born must assume for the family. This would be in keeping with the Biblical emphasis on 'responsibility', and its almost total silence on 'rights' in this sense: the employer is told of his responsibilities towards his employee but nothing of his rights as an employer, and similarly the employee is told of his responsibilities towards his employer, but nothing of his rights as an employee. So, also in the husband-wife relationship (Eph. 5:21–33; 6:5–9).

The respect the wife is exhorted to give to her husband is therefore to one who is not just the 'source of life' in a rudimentary, physical sense, but rather to one to whom has been committed the responsibility to care and provide for his family. Not that such responsibility of the husband precludes the co-operation and partnership of his wife, but that every team must have a captain, and, even though the captain is not the best player in the team, the team cannot function harmoniously unless the captain is allowed to perform the captain's role, and is fully supported in that role.

Conclusion

Genesis 1–2 give the foundation of a Biblical theology of sexuality, in the loving purpose of the Creator. The one word which could summarise that sexuality might be 'complementarity'. Genesis 3 comments theologically on the disharmony and state of rivalry between the sexes which is endemic in human society.

The New Testament gospel of Jesus Christ offers the path to a new harmony which can be achieved in the relationship between the sexes, as the Spirit of God does his work, through Christ and his example, of beginning the divine work of restoring in men and women the image of God so seriously marred.

TWO

ROMANS 1:24, 26, 27 AND THE MODERN SEXUALITY DEBATE

Geoffrey Grogan

This passage is crucial for the modern debate on homosexuality. In recent years, it has featured in the work of writers like John Boswell,[1] Robin Scroggs[2] and William Countryman[3] on the one hand, and Richard Hays,[4] David Wright[5] and Thomas Schmidt[6] on the other.

Boswell has argued that Paul is branding as sinful only homosexual acts committed by people with heterosexual orientation, Scroggs that what he condemns is aggressive pederasty and that there is no way of knowing what he would say about mutually consenting and committed homosexual relationships by people who have a natural homosexual orientation, and Countryman that he treats active homosexuality not as sin but as a form of ceremonial impurity and that Paul regarded such impurity as having no bearing on the conduct of Gentile Christians.

In their various ways, these three writers are united in asserting that Romans 1 cannot be used to brand such relationships today as sinful. It is well worth noting, however, that they are anything but agreed as to the way they interpret the passage. Is this significant? It might seem ungracious to suggest they are determined at all costs to evade the painful meaning of the passage, but there is surely at least a case to answer here!

Hays, Wright and Schmidt all criticise the exegesis on which these views are based, and they contend for a basically traditional exegesis of the passage.

At the outset, we should observe the call of Richard Hays for questions of exegesis and hermeneutics to be clearly distinguished.[7] [Exegesis—'the original meaning intended by Paul'; hermeneutics—'the significance of what Paul says for our problems today']. He is surely right. It is a serious error of method to approach the text immediately with modern issues in mind, reading it in their light. We need, first of all, to consider its meaning in its literary and historical setting. As Robin Scroggs says, 'Until we know what the biblical authors were against we cannot begin to reflect upon the relevance of those writings for contemporary issues'[8]. Hays criticises Boswell for failing to follow this methodology.

The meaning of the text for Paul and his first readers

(i) Paul writes to expound the gospel as the revelation of God's righteousness. Romans 1:16–7 is widely recognised as the key programmatic text of the epistle. For instance, J. C. Beker[9] holds that the theme of Romans revolves around four interrelated issues, all of which are found in these two verses. There has been much discussion of the purpose of the letter, but virtually all scholars treat this text as important in their assessment of the letter's main purpose.

If then we read the verses we are to consider in the light of 1:16, 17, this will mean that the human condition as it appears here is not necessarily final, so that the Gospel holds out hope to those who are caught up in sin. Its message of grace and therefore of divinely-given hope for the sinner should constantly be borne in mind.

(ii) Paul sees human history as the revelation of God's wrath in its reaction against human godlessness and unrighteousness. The positive exposition of the Gospel in terms of the righteousness of God commences at Romans 3:21. Prior to this, Paul deals with the revelation of God's wrath against human godlessness and unrighteousness. It is particularly important to see that this passage is not simply about sin but about the way God's wrath is revealed against it. This makes its theme a very solemn one.

Paul views God's wrath as revealed both historically and eschatologically. The eschatological dimen-
sion of his wrath and judgment is seen in 2:1–16 and
3:5–8, the historical in 1:18–32. Paul uses the present
continuous tense of *apocaluptein* ('reveal') in 1:18 and
most of the verbs in the passage that follow this are in
the aorist, so that he appears to contemplating the whole
of human history including its contemporary phase,
without of course making reference to particular events.

So he is not writing about individual sin but rather
about the disclosure of God's wrath in the whole human story. We should note that his threefold use of
paradidomi ('give up') in verses 24, 26, 28 is consist-
ently in the aorist, which is of course the most natural
tense for historical discourse. F. F. Bruce appropriately
quotes a saying of Schiller, 'The history of the world is
the judgment of the world'.[10]

The historical nature of this passage is in fact in line
with the historical concentration of Romans, for passages like 3:19–26, 4:1–25, 5:12–21, 8:18–25 and chapters 9 to 11 are all historical or historical/eschatological
in form.

(iii) He sees sin as the result of God's wrath as well as
its cause. The way *paradidomi* is used here shows this
clearly. Verses 18–23 look like an exposition of 'godlessness' and verses 24–32 of 'unrighteousness'. It is
at the start of this second section that this verb is em-
ployed for the first time. It attributes what follows to

the reprobating activity of God. Humanity's wilful rebellion against the light of creation concerning the nature of God is the moral cause of this reprobating activity, so that this godlessness becomes the cause of unrighteousness.

The phrase *godlessness and unrighteousness* functions as a kind of rubric covering all that follows to the end of the chapter. It is not easy, therefore, on contextual grounds, to agree to Countryman's reduction of terms normally understood to be ethical (and so related to sin) so that they become ceremonial (and so related to purity).

Thomas E. Schmidt has also shown the lexical basis of Countryman's argument cannot bear investigation, and that at least eight of the terms used in the key verses should be understood ethically. We cannot pursue his arguments[11] in detail here, but it is worth noting that he maintains, surely correctly, that if even one of them is ethical, this crucial part of Countryman's argument falls. His one concession to Countryman is that *plane*, at the close of verse 27, ought to be seen as a theological rather than an ethical term and translated *error* (AV, RSV) rather than *perversion* (NIV).

(iv) He views the moral exchange involved in homosexuality as an appropriate penalty for the theological exchange involved in idolatry. Paul uses *allasso* in verse 23 and its compound *metallasso* in verses 25 and 26, both normally translated 'exchange'. His use in particular of the compound verb in consecutive verses, first of all with reference to idolatry and then to homosexuality, surely implies some parallel between the theological and moral errors, in fact, because of the use of *paradidomi* ('give up') between them, that the second is an appropriate penalty for the first.

This understanding of the passage is strengthened when we note Paul's use of *physicen* ('natural') in verses 26 and 27. Cranfield says, 'By "natural" and "contrary to nature" Paul clearly means "in accordance with the Creator's intention" and "contrary to the Creator's intention" respectively'.

The context shows a number of important linguistic parallels with the Septuagint (the Greek translation) of Genesis 1. Cranfield's further comment is therefore appropriate when he says, 'It is not impossible that Paul had some awareness of the great importance which "nature" had in Greek thought for centuries; that he was aware of its use in contemporary popular philosophy is very likely. But the decisive factor in his use of it is his biblical doctrine of creation'.[12]

Is Paul's language restricted to homosexual activity which was closely linked to idolatry and was part of pagan worship? No, for when he writes of *the lusts of their hearts* (v.24), *dishonorable passions* (v.26), and of people being *consumed with passion* (v.27) he is using pejorative language which is distinctly ethical rather than religious.

To apply this language simply to heterosexuals acting against their nature by committing homosexual acts is to commit gross anachronism, for it assumes a distinction between 'natural' and 'unnatural' homosexuality which was totally foreign to all thinking, whether Jewish, Greek or Roman, at the time when Paul was writing.

Certainly, pederasty was the common form of homosexuality in Paul's day, but the wider bearing of his language becomes clear, as David Wright has pointed out, when we see that he includes female homosexual activity too.[13] This was very little recorded in Paul's world and yet he makes reference to it in parallel terms to male behaviour. Can there be any doubt that he intended to make blanket reference to homosexual activity as such as being contrary to the Creator's intention and therefore sinful?

(v) Conclusion as to Paul's meaning in this passage. Paul is here indicating that homosexual activity, both male and female, and without further distinction, is contrary to the Creator's intention, that its existence in the world is an appropriate penalty for the worship of elements of the creation instead of the Creator, and that it is therefore a manifestation of his present wrath, which will be finally revealed at the day of judgment. There is however hope if sinful human beings will put their faith (a penitent faith, as Rom. 6:1ff. implies) in God through Christ.

Application of the passage to the current debate

If the passage refers to all homosexual activity without distinction and regards it as contrary to the Creator's intention and therefore as both a manifestation of his present wrath and subject to the final revelation of that wrath in eschatological judgment, the question of its application today is highly important.

Paul's teaching here is closely related to teaching of fundamental importance in Biblical theology. If Paul is a consistent writer, with the Christian *kerygma* ('proclamation', i.e. 'what is proclaimed', 'the message') as the factor which gives integration to all he says, this kerygmatic basis of his thought is never more evident than it is in this epistle. Romans 1:16-7 is one of the clearest brief statements of that *kerygma* in his extant writings, and the letter itself is Paul's *magnum opus* on the nature and implications, both theological and ethical, of that *kerygma*.

Moreover, he is writing to a church where he has not yet laboured, and yet, at least in this section of the epistle, he apparently sees no need to argue for the position he takes, strongly suggesting that it was common to that apostolic teaching which was normative for all the churches.

In addition, his thought is grounded in the Old Testament, and not simply in the outlook of contemporary Judaism. As Hays has pointed out,[14] there may be an allusion to Leviticus 18:22 and 20:13 in Romans 1:32, but the chief O.T. background is to be found in the basic creation theology of Genesis 1. This creation theology reappears, not only in Psalm 8, Ecclesiastes, in so-called Deutero-Isaiah and in many other parts of the Old Testament, but, even more importantly, also in the teaching, including the ethical teaching, of Jesus. It is identifiable as part of what C. H. Dodd, in *According to the Scriptures*, calls the sub-structure of New Testament theology.

For all these reasons, it would seem impossible to hold, with George Edwards,[15] that Paul is simply giving an account of conventional Jewish attitudes towards Gentiles in order to set up his later rejection of Jewish self-righteousness.

It is true that the New Testament has little teaching on the homosexual issue, but teaching such as Paul gives here, which relates to such central themes of New Testament and Old Testament theology, is thereby given an importance which makes its rejection serious if we have desire to be Biblical Christians.

New Testament Christian ethics affirm Old Testament ethics when these are related to the creation order. It might of course be argued that the Mosaic legislation does not necessarily apply to Christians. Paul's use of the language of Genesis 1, however, grounds his teaching in the created order. In particular, verse 23, which refers to *images resembling mortal man or birds or animals or reptiles* (RSV) uses Greek words all but one of which (the exception is *mortal*), are to be found in Genesis 1:20–6. The Jews have always placed special emphasis on the relevance of the creation order and the Noachian ordinances for human life generally and this would appear to be sound and an approach with which Christians can identify.

In discussing the Mosaic legislation, Paul argues from the temporal priority of the Abrahamic covenant (Gal. 3:15–8). Even more significantly, in an ethical discussion, Jesus himself argued from the temporal priority of the teaching of Genesis 2 about marriage (Matt. 19:8–9). Moreover, family relationships, which in Scripture go right back to early Genesis, are of central importance in New Testament ethical teaching.

In the creation narratives fundamental issues concerning the nature of God, of human beings and of their relationship to each other are in view, and this material forms the basic framework for all that the Bible writers say about that relationship both in terms of divine judgment and of divine redemption.

We cannot reckon any form of homosexual behaviour to be exempt from the strictures of this passage. This follows from Paul's grounding of his thought in the created order. In fact, he sees human nature to be deeply affected by sin, and, if there is now such a thing as 'natural homosexuality', there can be little doubt that he would regard this as itself part of the global consequences of humanity's departure from God. As Hays points out, 'Paul's condemnation of homosexual activity does not rest on an assumption that it is freely chosen; indeed it is precisely characteristic of Paul to regard "sin" as a condition of human existence, a condition which robs us of free volition and drives us to disobedient actions which, though involuntary, are nonetheless culpable (see especially Rom. 7:13–25). That is what it means to live "in the flesh" in a fallen creation'.[16]

There are no Biblical grounds for regarding homosexuality as 'the sin of sins', and the sensitive Christian, recognising his or her own sinfulness, will feel a deep pastoral concern for the person struggling with homosexuality and the special problems that person faces, while, in faithfulness to Scripture, treating all homosexual genital activity as contrary to God's creative intention and therefore as sinful.

As Paul's thought is grounded in the creation order, we cannot reckon any form of homosexual behaviour exempt from the strictures of this passage. Also, however, the Christian both believes from Scripture and knows in personal experience the grace of God to sinners and so can bring a wonderful message of hope to the penitent.

THREE

SOME ISSUES RAISED BY THE HOMOSEXUALITY DEBATE

David Wright

Of one thing we may be sure: challenging issues about sexual relationships other than (heterosexual) marriage will not go away, whatever the General Assembly of the Church of Scotland or any church organ decides. The reason for this is simple—that the acceptance of such relationships is widespread in our society, and in particular has deep roots in influential areas of British culture, both popular and more sophisticated.

Another reason is more worrying: some of the opinion-formers within the mainstream churches seem to view these developments almost as bearers of fresh wisdom from God. The social realities of sexual behaviour are no longer, it seems, to be evaluated in the light of God's once-for-all self-revelation in Christ; they may even be held to constitute norms which the churches ignore at their peril. As a recent Archbishop of York once put it, unless the Church of England changes its mind on divorce, it will lose touch with the people—as though the latter is more to be feared than departing from what that Church believes to be the mind of God. Such an attitude informs many a revisionist approach to these questions, even if it is not expressed in such naked terms.

We may expect, therefore, that Christians who see no reason to abandon traditional teaching grounded in Scripture will increasingly find themselves swimming against the tide. The Christian lifestyle will become more and more counter-cultural, and because of the growing acceptance, in sectors of mixed denominations, of sub-Christian patterns of behaviour (as they have hitherto been universally regarded), internal church divisions are likely to widen. The cohesiveness of a body like the Church of Scotland will surely be tested as never before—if (which God forbid) it tolerates elders living together outside marriage or practising homosexuals pairing off in the manse.

Pastors and teachers who are sensitive to the signs of the times will already be equipping their congregations, especially at the younger end, to live against the stream. I sometimes wonder if ministers are direct or explicit enough in their teaching on sexual morality. A proper modesty may have its place, but sometimes too much is taken for granted. Why is it that from time to time students turn up in university CUs never having heard that sex outside marriage is wrong? It is an odd situation if every other means of communication that influences our lives calls a spade a spade apart from the pulpit.

Moreover, we have to be ready with more than straight affirmation. The arguments of the revisionists must be shown to be wanting. What follows will attempt to provide some guidance for this task.

Relationships: values versus form?

It is often said that what matters is not the structure of a relationship, but the qualities that inform it. What gives it integrity are virtues like trust, openness, commitment and acceptance, irrespective of whether it conforms to God's design. Much better, so it is claimed, a partnership that displays these values, whether heterosexual or homosexual, than a loveless shrivelled marriage. As countless pop songs put it, love is all you need—scarcely different from the 'new morality' of a generation ago (John Robinson, Harry Williams *et al.*) which opposed love to law and first taught Christians that sex outside marriage might, with love, be OK. (What a fearful responsibility that 'new morality' generation bears for our present disorders!)

If we take our bearings from Scripture, this is a false choice. Divinely ordered relationships and God-given qualities belong together. The fact that some marriages go sour is no warrant for dispensing with marriage. There is no basis in Scripture for believing that love and other Christian qualities justify or hallow an improper relationship. It is undeniable that cohabiting couples may show deep and selfless affection for each other, and that a 'gay' partnership may be marked by enviable mutual care. (We have no interest in rubbishing all such relationships as fired by selfish gratification.) But they fall short in varying degrees of God's plan for one-to-one relationships in which alone is sexual fulfilment to be found. Honour among thieves may be truly admirable, but it does not sanction thieving.

Starting at the beginning: the heterosexual norm

There are few things as fundamental in the biblical revelation as the divine ordering of heterosexual monogamy. It is found throughout Scripture—for example, in two of the Ten Commandments, in the teaching of Jesus, where it is reaffirmed and its implications deepened, and in Ephesians as an image of the love between Christ and his church. To excise or override this foundation is to do deep structural damage to the teaching of Scripture. And if it is objected that Jesus, the perfect human being, was not married, that very fact marked him out as destined for a highly exceptional calling among his contemporaries.

We must refuse to let go of this starting point. Too many discussion documents from churches in recent years have begun elsewhere—with a general or common sexuality celebrated as God's gift. Only later do they go on to consider the proper expressions of this sexuality. But the Bible knows nothing of an undifferentiated or abstract sexuality, which may be exercised in different ways. From start to finish it presents heterosexuality—men created as sexual beings for sexual matching with women, and women likewise for men. To abandon this basis (which is embodied in the differing anatomies of male and female) is to set off on the wrong foot at the outset.

So the biblical case for disapproving of homosexual conduct does not rest on a few contested texts, but on a widely pervasive feature of the revealed wisdom of God for human life. Yet the explicit New Testament references (Rom. 1:26–27, 1 Cor. 6:9) carry a heavier punch than revisionists allow. (See my Cutting Edge series booklet *The Christian Faith and Homosexuality*, and more fully my article in *Evangelical Quarterly* 61, 1989, pp. 291–300, 'Homosexuality: the Relevance of the Bible'. The best book on the whole issue is Thomas E. Schmidt, *Straight and Narrow? Compassion and Clarity in the Homosexuality Debate*, from IVP.)

Not forgetting the Fall

Against this backcloth of God's creative blueprint, the many distortions of sexual disposition and behaviour in human society have to be understood in terms of the fallenness of all humankind. In the case of homosexuality, this applies to orientation as well as to behaviour, and this will not change if or when a genetic explanation for the homosexual condition is discovered.

There is no mileage in denying or resisting the iden-
tification of genetic factors as wholly or partly respon-
sible for homosexual tendencies. To do otherwise would
be to take refuge in something like God-of-the-gaps
theology in reverse, as though only in the gaps in current genetic science could one discern the effects of the
Fall.

It is no new challenge for biblical Christians to regard deeply ingrained inclinations or orientations in
men and women, whether genetically caused or not, as
part of the detritus of the fallenness of the race. In this
respect, as in others, homosexuality must not be iso-
lated either from the reach of basic Christian beliefs or
from other comparable conditions, such as alcohol-
ism, kleptomania or paedophilia.

Loving the sinner, hating the sin

This sounds glib and facile, and is often resented by
'gay' lobbyists as insulting. Yet it is surely, as a general
phrase, no more—and no less!—than what the core
message of Christianity is all about! If the mission of
Jesus, and the reason why the incarnate Son was given
this human name, was to save us from our sins, then
not only the distinction between sinner and their sins
but also the separation of one from the other lie at the
heart of things. Again, this approach to homosexuality
sets it in the context of the gospel which encompasses
'all sorts and conditions of men'. I emphasize this point

in the face of denials, implicit or explicit, that homosexuals need, or can benefit from, the central message
of the Christian gospel, which summons us all—or
rather, only sinners, not the righteous!—to faith and
repentance.

Human identity—in creation and in Christ

One reason why revisionists resent 'love the sinner,
hate the sin' is that they treat homosexuality as consti-
tutive of a person's identity. Talk of sundering a man or
woman from his or her homosexuality is thus felt as a
threat to their essential being. What they demand is
acceptance specifically as 'gay' or lesbian.

This sense of hurt calls for a sensitive response. It
may well be the case that when we talk about homosexuality in any public gathering, one or more of those
listening will feel that their whole being is under challenge. We need to be aware of this possibility, without
accepting the assumptions and instincts it represents.
It may be understandable, in a society so preoccupied
with (heterosexual) sexual fulfilment as ours appears
to be, why persons of different sexual disposition should
perceive their identity so much in terms of this difference.

But it is surely far healthier to insist that our worth
as human beings consists in our being created in God's
image and recreated in Christ. No higher value can be
placed on a man or woman than this. It is a particularly
worrying feature of the 'gay' and lesbian Christian

movement that it seeks recognition of homosexuals precisely in terms of their homosexuality, instead of as creatures of God, sinful like all of us but capable of being remade in Christ. Others do not rest their personal identity in their heterosexuality!

Acceptance and non-acceptance

The domination of late-twentieth-century liberal Christianity by an almost antinomian inclusivism is reflected in the way 'acceptance' has ousted 'forgiveness'. Forgiveness recognizes, and acceptance often implicitly denies, the need for repentance. Christ accepts us as sinners, but accepts us in forgiveness, not in mere recognition that we are who we are. And where there is room for forgiveness (and there is no acceptance by God without it), there is room for hearts and lives to be changed. Jesus refused to condemn the adulteress to the punishment Jewish law required, but his acceptance of her accompanied a sharp summons to abandon her adultery. Much the same can be said of the use of 'affirm' (except that grammatically it is much odder to say 'the gospel affirms me'!).

Evangelical churches above all others should be places where the good news of a forgiving and welcoming God is heard in unmistakeable tones by sinners of all kinds—including the notorious offenders of the Gospels. But there is no hint in the Gospels that Jesus approved or tolerated prostitutes continuing to ply their trade or taxgatherers continuing to fleece taxpayers. The Scottish Reformed tradition has probably erred in the direction of legalism, but this is no excuse for swinging to the other extreme of cheap grace that makes no moral demands and expects no moral renewal.

Reading the Bible whole: or, against separating what God has joined together

The revisionist liberalism that is now ready to accept nonmarital heterosexual and same-sex relationships often seems a throwback to the Jesus-only liberalism of an earlier era. The Old Testament and Paul are largely pensioned off as incurably patriarchal, in an exclusive appeal to the Jesus of the Gospels. Yet even this is not free from selectivity—citing John 8:11a but omitting John 8:11b. A church in the Reformed tradition should be the last to excise the Old Testament from the Bible like Marcion, if it is faithful to its true genius.

It is difficult to take seriously as an argument in favour of accepting homosexual behaviour that Jesus said nothing about it. If this is indeed the case, it would not be surprising. Jesus said nothing about a great many topics that were not live issues in Palestine in his day—like social security schemes, democracy and votes for all, and equal pay for women (and even about many that presumably were, like nationalism, housing the homeless, disarmament and the care of the terminally ill). And it is agreed that homosexuality became an issue for the Jews only when they spread into the Hel-

lenistic world (just as earlier it had been an issue for
Israel only when encountered among its Canaanite
neighbours).

This argument from the silence of Jesus is a kind of
negative proof texting—and reflects a naively
unhistorical treatment of the Gospels. As such, it is
another instance of the arbitrary selectivity that the revisionist case relies on throughout: it severely restricts
the relevance of the Old Testament and most of the
New Testament apart from the Gospels on the grounds
of their historical relativism (they reflect the social and
cultural worlds in which they originated), but asks questions of the Gospels in a totally non-historical fashion.
If any of the Bible is historically conditioned, all of it
is. There is no core-gospel (not even 'God is love')
which comes to us except in a particular vocabulary
(first-century Greek in this case), from a particular context (that of 1 John, its author and recipients). 'God is
love' is true in a biblical sense, *i.e.* as biblically war-
ranted, only when 'God' and 'love' are given their first-
century contextualised meanings—not as any modern
might care to conceive of God and love!

Note well: the sound response to 'But that's all
patriarchalism!' is not to try to carve out some reserved
territory free of this plague, but to insist that there is no
self-revelation of God except that given under such
socio-cultural limitations. Jesus was not incarnate except as a Jew in first-century Palestine, nor crucified
except 'under Pontius Pilate', and the New Testament

comes to us only in Hellenistic Greek. We either accept—and glory in!—the scandal of particularity, or set about creating our own religion in embarrassment at the once-for-all givenness of historic Christianity.

So the debate about homosexuality turns out to encapsulate a number of the critical issues in the battle to hold on to a Christianity that is recognisably the faith of our mothers and fathers. The alternative is a faith that is made in our own image, and made anew in every generation. But of a faith in which we see the reflection, narcissistically, of our contemporary society's values and aspirations, one thing is sure—it cannot save contemporary society. A gospel read off even the best of today's insights and wisdom will be so different (a gospel) that it will not be (another) gospel at all (see Galatians 1:6–7).

FOUR

A PASTORAL PERSPECTIVE ON THE PROBLEMS OF OUR FALLEN SEXUALITY

William Still

Sexuality is an inherent part of human nature with its own unique drive in mature and maturing adults. It is astonishing, therefore, that its legitimate sphere, as far as the Bible is concerned, is laid down as only within the confines of marriage—the joining of man and woman together in sexual union. This virtually excludes overt sexual experience as a relevant, moral subject for the celibate.

Freud and others have tried to show that sex increases human happiness, but an article in *The Times* in January 1993[1] said simply that sex results in great unhappiness as people vainly try to live up to the ideal. And when sex doesn't bring joy and pleasure, says Liz Hodgkinson in this article, we can start to blame and even hate the partner—or ourselves. She says:

> Many people discover that their physical health
> improves during a time of voluntary celibacy. This

is because sex brings into play a large amount of stress hormones, which can eventually lead to stress-related diseases. Although a life of celibacy is popularly imagined to be one of misery, deprivation and continual frustration and repression, it can be the very opposite, and provide a wonderful opportunity to get to know yourself, understand who you are and what is your real purpose in life. It can also allow to develop hitherto undiscovered talents. A period of voluntary celibacy can give space and time to become autonomous and self-sufficient. It can bestow a powerful feeling of liberation and lightness. It means you can truly reclaim yourself, and become free from the sexual demands of your own body and also the sexual desires of other people, which you may not always feel like accommodating.

Well, are you wondering if you are reading aright? It's a change, you must agree, from most that we hear, read or see about sex these days. Most evocative, if not provocative enough for a celibate (like myself) to gloat over it shockingly! Nonetheless, sex is undoubtedly a dominating factor in human life, directly and indirectly; it relates to, and affects, practically every sphere of adult life, so much so that any tampering with its potential in childhood is almost bound to have a deleterious effect upon growing children, and may injure the whole of their subsequent adult life.

The problems are legion

One is obliged to ask, 'How are we to regard sexuality in its general effect on human life?' Some might suggest the answer is marriage. But even within marriage, its problems are legion, as every pastor will testify.

For example, withholding conjugal rights, for whatever reason—whether incompatibility, or because of undue sexual demands—can lead to such temptation to the other spouse towards unlawful extra-marital relations as to be a frequent source of sexual immorality. Therefore, to seek for sexual, as well as spiritual, moral, intellectual, and emotional, compatibility is a high responsibility in a world in which there is such diversity of human nature.

In a fallen world, it is far from surprising that so many individuals either never find sexual harmony, or having found it, regard it so lightly that the sinful questing of their personality looks for extra-marital sexual experience. The result is inevitably the disordering of at least three lives, and often many more, especially where offspring are involved.

Marriage breakdown

The possibilities of sexual incompatibility or misalliance are so infinite that it would seem a miracle that any, or certainly many, should find complete harmony in marriage; hence sexual immorality must be one of the greatest moral problems known to man. The marvel is that so many do find sexual harmony and pro-

duce children, and that then these children themselves
in turn find sexual compatibility within the lawful canons of biblical morality. Our concern in this article is
with those who don't!

Even amongst professing Christians, advocates of
Christianity, and the 'professionally religious', marriage breakdowns occur too frequently. If for the ma-
jority of souls there is a marital partner to be found
within their normal daily orbit—and bear in mind that
many are often obliged to make do with the best available—this surely calls for nothing less than divine guidance from him who knows all.

Divine canons

In the midst of the infinite variety of the problems of
sexual immorality, the canons of biblical guidance and
restraint are such that, where they are acknowledged
and observed, they limit the injury that can be inflicted
on the human personality. But that requires a high degree of both morality and spirituality.

To commit oneself wholly to Christ, for him to govern the totality of one's life, will mean that his help will
be enlisted in, at least, damage limitation. A very great
deal can be done in that sphere where the presence,
help and comfort of the Lord is sought to achieve containment of one's sexual desires within the necessary
restraints which need to govern distressing experiences
of non-satisfaction.

It is in such situations that an involvement and encounter with the living Christ can make all the difference between the immoral ruin of a life which finds itself the victim of unhappy, unfulfilled sexual experience, or a life which finds approximate fulfilment and satisfaction within the constraints of happy sexual experience. A person who (for whatever reason) has been divorced, or bereaved of a spouse, is for a season (at least), deprived of sexual fulfilment. He or she needs special grace, as well as the prayers of sympathetic Christian friends, to prove the value of restraint under biblical laws. And to find, perhaps temporarily, a lifestyle in which the sexual drive finds other than sexual outlets and expressions than formerly.

Spiritual and moral help

Of course, all who have not found sexual compatibility in marriage need spiritual and moral help. The frustration of sexual desire is a major experience in any life, and there is no end to the forms of counsel which could be offered to persons in such situations. Certainly those who have known sexual satisfaction to some extent and then for some reason have been deprived of it, need very special help. They suffer such a profound loss that nothing but the understanding of a loving heavenly Father and his incarnate Son can assuage. The solution may be another lawful sexual union. It may also be commitment to a life of self-denial in which the good Lord is almost bound to provide some other direction for a now frustrated and unfulfilled urge.

When one thinks of the infinite possibilities of sexual maladjustment, it is of all things, the possibility of friendship with the Lord Jesus which is by far the greatest factor in finding solutions to such problems. Indeed, in these circumstances there can be few as comforting words as those which say, 'Like as a father pities his children, so the Lord pities them that fear him. For he knows our frame; he remembers that we are dust'.

It can only be the enemy of souls who keeps Christian people from giving wholehearted attention to such a comforting promise. As in so much of the Christian life, peace and satisfaction are found in keeping the enemy and his nefarious tricks at bay to permit us to enjoy the Lord and his satisfactions, whatever other satisfactions may be withheld from us.

Containment and re-direction

That being the case, there is a sexuality which finds its exercise and fulfilment in what may be called re-direction, that is, not in physical sexual satisfaction as such. It must be said that, contrary to what some carnal spirits would allege, sexual containment is far from injurious to life, but can be a blessing in disguise, because its drive may be re-directed towards other, higher satisfactions. The chiefest of those is the affection which should accompany all sexual experience, but which can be expressed ad infinitum where there is no possibility of physical sexual experience, yet where that affectionate regard which is the essence of good sexual relations can be expressed with absolutely no sexual arousal at all.

This is not to say that sexual feeling ceases to exist. Far from it. But it must be admitted that it thereafter takes a considerably lesser place in one's reckoning than formerly. Is this not a great advantage, providing at least a partial solution to sexual frustration? There is this other way! An alternative indeed, which *The Times* article, quoted above, discussed, and a way which the stormy sexual passions of the carnally demanding souls simply have not found.

And surely this is the way we must approach the problems of all who are sexually deprived, whatever their sexual problems may be.

Where that deprivation is within the marriage bond on account of the sinful withholding of lawful marital rights by one spouse from the other, study 1 Corinthians 7:3-7 to see what God says about mutual obligations. The limitation prescribed by the seventh commandment with regard to adultery, and the warnings in the pastoral Epistles with regard to continence within the marriage bond (1Tim. 2:2-12; 5:9; Tit 1:6), indicate that this frustration needs to be borne continentally within the realms of grace. Within those realms there are always such divine compensations as the goodness of God in his grace may be pleased to provide (*e.g.* 1 Sam. 1:8).

Fortunately, the Scriptures as indicated above are

wonderfully explicit about problems within the marriage bond. Outside the marriage bond, however, it must be admitted that there is less help. Most of it is of a negative nature, which again is natural because outside the bonds of marriage the physical sexual urge clearly has no legitimate area of expression. The highest which is offered is containment, or re-direction towards some other legitimate area of satisfaction and of affectionate service of others.

Perhaps the celibate lives of the heterosexual, bisexual or homosexual individual in a Christian and biblical context are basically not so very different from each other. Some kind of subliminal continence is surely the worthy goal, along with that patience which divine grace may afford, which looks to the Lord for any further relationships which might offer legitimate satisfactions.

A marriage partner

What might such further relationships be? For the heterosexual (and for the bisexual who with growing maturity may tend to lean toward the heterosexual side), there is always the possibility that the good Lord will provide a helpmeet.

For the homosexual and bisexual who on maturing find that there is still a leaning toward the homosexual side, the matter is not so easily solved. Indeed, let it never be thought that it is beyond the powers of the Almighty, by whatever means, to correct a preponderantly homosexual urge. Although such an urge can be, and often is, exceedingly deep-seated, it will take a work of singular grace and power to dismantle and demolish the sexual feelings of years to replace them with heterosexual feelings.

A loving Father

Let it therefore now be stated, that, since we are evidently in realms of often excruciating personal spiritual and emotional agonies, it is imperative the sufferer seeks the constant comforting guidance of a loving heavenly Father. Nothing less can keep a person with a seemingly innate perverted sexual urge from seeking those opportunities for illegitimate satisfactions of which in our modern, godless society there are too many.

Hope is said to spring eternal in the human breast. It is natural for those disoriented sexually to long for sexual satisfaction. When with maturer years neither a legitimate solution to the problem, nor a radical or miracle cure of perverted feelings has been found, it may be necessary to conclude that it is the good Lord's will that life should be lived within that deprivation. Those faced with that prospect need to know clearly that grace will be given to bear the prohibition, lawfully and bravely, and that in God's kindness he will be pleased to provide some sort of alternative subliminal satisfaction. The legitimate affectionate outlets of a caring kind, for those deprived of sexual gratification, are endless, although such souls may well feel that even at best these are poor alternatives to that which is biblically forbidden.

Biblical prohibitions challenged

That the Scriptures are against homosexual practice there can be no doubt, and the conviction that this is true and right simply grows with every futile attempt made to re-interpret biblical statements in both Testaments to allow such practice. The growing trend of such re-interpretation seen in the work of men such as John Boswell, Robin Scroggs and William Countryman,[2] has had its effect on some within Scotland—witness the Church of Scotland's Panel on Doctrine Report to the 1994 General Assembly.

Pastoral counselling

The most important thing to do with any soul who is to any extent torn between natural and unnatural sexual desire is to try to help them discourage the unnatural, and chastely to increase and normalise whatever heterosexual inclinations they may have. That can take years! That is why we should never brand anyone irrevocably homosexual under a certain age. We must give ample time under guidance to see whether with increasing maturity and the pursuance of natural sexual feelings they may be able to right themselves. Or at least to mortify the perverse element, if not extirpate it altogether.

A most encouraging fact is the number of men who, having passed through a seemingly homosexual stage, have emerged into heterosexuality sufficiently to contemplate marriage, and in marriage and family life have found a solution to their problem enough to make life tolerable and stable. It needs to be said, however, that homosexual feelings may still arise, especially in susceptible encounters. But by grace these experiences may be successfully mortified, so that normal married and family life goes on, whether the spouse knows about the other's problem or not. (Some women are able to cope with the knowledge of their husbands' tendencies. Whereas some can hardly bear to know about them at all. Of course, abhorrence can stem from an unrealistic and unwisely idealistic attitude towards the hazards of human life. We are all sinners, and pharisaical sinners are surely the worst. See Jesus about that!)

On the other hand, some have precipitately entered into marriage in the hope that their problem of disorientated sexuality would thereby be solved, and many pastors have seen how hopeless that can be. It all depends on the degree of bias towards one sex or the other. This situation generally needs to be pastorally monitored over a period of months and even years, to see where the bias eventually may lean. If it continues increasingly to be on the homosexual side, the worst possible advice would be to marry! That has ruined many lives and broken the hearts of many men and women.

The confirmed homosexual

Now turn to the confirmed homosexual. We must return to the basic fact that God hates what is unnatural,
and nothing can make him change his mind about the
abuse of the natural functions he has ordained for man
as for his other creatures. That is why what is called
'unisex' is so abominable, and the desire of women to
look like men and behave like men, and men to dress
and develop natural characteristics such as excessive
hair so as to look like and behave like a woman, is
absolutely abhorrent to God and ought to be deplored
by the godly.

This must be where we start, whoever may be hurt.
But I want to appeal for a new degree of understanding. I have in view those who, through no fault of their
own, are afflicted with perverse desires, and may be
cruelly hounded to the point of suicide by a misguided
use of the name of God and Christ. On their behalf, one
must register a protest and complete condemnation of
a judgmentalism which utterly ignores the infinite understanding of the holy Jesus, who, although he never
excuses sin but must ever condemn it, always loves the
sinner. 'Neither do I condemn you; go, and sin no more',
shows the perfect balance of Christ's attitude towards
all sin, but with particular reference to sexual sin.

We must distinguish between the deliberate perver-
sity of heterosexual sinners in experimenting with ho-

mosexuality purely for 'kicks', and the sins of those who grow up with, or are seduced into homosexual inclinations and acts which then become more natural to them than the natural. Such unnatural sins, whether committed by heterosexual experimenters, or by those hooked on homosexuality, can never be excused or exonerated, nor used to overturn the biblical stance (as some are increasingly seeking to do).

Christian compassion

In the interests of the compassion of Jesus Christ, there needs to be a far greater degree of understanding of why people do these things, however rightly disapproving we must be of their acts. Jesus' understanding of the woman of Samaria, the woman taken in adultery and Zacchaeus (a very different case), shows us how sad it is that in biblical, Christian, and evangelical circles there can be so much harsh, cruel and ruthless dismissal of problem people. Too often, not the slightest attempt is made to understand why they behave as they do, or to bring them to our blessed Lord's touchstone, 'Neither do I condemn thee; go and sin no more'.

Our concern here is for those who for whatever reason and at whatever stage in their development have become so completely warped and twisted that to them the natural has become unnatural and the unnatural natural. It is ours to help them see that this is the work of the devil in their lives. Just as some are born spina bifida or with other physical malformations, there are those who are either born with, or quickly acquire and develop, unnatural tendencies to the exclusion of the natural. This leads to their revulsion against what is natural. Short of a miraculous transformation by grace, they need to be helped to accept their thorn in the flesh, as Paul did, as a cross to be accepted for Christ's sake and used for his glory. Some of the most gifted people in the world in various realms have owed their God-used gift to the drive of sexual abnormality which has been accepted as an affliction (permitted by God, though obviously attributable to fallen human nature), to be to a degree sublimated, transformed and used to the glory of God.

Godly sublimation

I have known those who were faced with extreme temptation to 'unnatural sin' who so resolutely refused to succumb to what fatally attracted them but which they knew was wrong, that I was astonished. But on reflection, I knew why their aesthetic, pastoral, and preaching gifts were signally used of God. That very drive which could have ruined them was used, when transmogrified into an instrument of God, as the means of saving and blessing many.

But let me emphasise again, that all such godly sublimation of seemingly innate sexual abnormality must be accepted and given over to God for death and transformation. This can only be done when the tendency has been recognised as a fault and flaw and not as another kind of normality! It is therefore to be mortified with a view to seeing how the Lord will re-channel its drive, if intractable, towards something to be used by God. It could then become as beautiful as the fruit of those to whom the gift of natural union is given.

Not only in the realms of artistic endeavour, but in those of loving relationships, especially in the befriending and helping of needy souls, God has used people who endure agonisingly painful deviant tendencies, but who have given their maladjustment to him for transformation. This is true of far more than many who are rigidly moralistic in the Christian world would believe! Some people hold up their hands in holy horror at even hearing that so and so has such a problem. But if they knew how sympathetic the Lord is to the affliction, and how he stands ready to use it when it is given to him, they might be shocked out of their self-righteousness.

Jesus is far more daring in what he does and whom he employs than many exceedingly pious souls dare to believe. Perhaps that's why hypocrites don't like to get too near him. He's a shocker!

The cost

But the cost to such suffering souls! Who can compute it? What the so-called incurable homosexual soul endures in loneliness and unfulfilled longing is something which long experience of sharing with such souls has taught me to be nothing less than an excruciating agony. If there is one thing such souls need above all, it is counsel on two fronts: first, that affliction with an unnatural propensity, which can only come from Satan—by whatever means is beside the point—has to be accepted; and, second, like Paul's thorn in the flesh, it has to be given over to God for him to transform. This can be done through grace when it is sublimated into something beautiful and wonderfully useful to him. In short, what we pastors must do is to face the biblical truth about such tendencies and then, accepting that they are warps and twists, seek God's help to find for such souls, if there is to be no cure, a true sublimation and outlet which is both approved and blessed by God.

At the same time we ought to see to it that we make the sacrificial lot of these souls as comfortable as possible. Perhaps frustrated Christian counsellors should find it in their hearts to pray, that it might be in the divine will for such people to find someone with whom a friendship can be formed and a level of association maintained which helps in bearing each other's burden in Christ, according to Christ's rules of purity.

FIVE

ONE HOMOSEXUAL'S VIEW

There are not insignificant numbers of us in the Church who have a homosexual orientation and, at the same time, are anxious to keep faith with God and to maintain biblical integrity by refusing to give physical expression to our same-sex preferences, however difficult it may be at times. We accept the message of holy Scripture in its condemnation of all homosexual acts as wrong and against God's revealed will, although such views may go against the grain of much secular thought and practice and leave us open to charges of obscurantism along with the verbal attacks of gay activists.

We reject the modern Kinsey with his crude findings that 'everyone is doing it', thereby sanctioning homosexuality as a normal alternative lifestyle, as well as the ancient Socrates arguing that homosexuality is a superior form of human love because it unites 'the love of a beautiful body with the love of a beautiful soul'. We challenge the wisdom of any of our contemporaries—however well-meaning—who advocate or endorse what is described as faithful and permanent ho-

mosexual love between Christians. Such partnerships
are alien to the whole tenor of the Bible where there is
neither commendation nor instructions for same-sex
relationships. We have taken to heart the truth of God's
Word in passages such as 1 Corinthians 6:9–10 and 1
Timothy 1:10 in its prohibition of active homosexual
encounters of all kinds. As Christian believers, we hon-
estly seek to interpret our predilection in the light of
Scripture rather than interpret Scripture in the light of
our predilection.

In such an attitude of mind we approach Paul's epistle to the Corinthians, for example, acknowledging that
while he does certainly classify homosexual acts as
sinful he does not disdainfully single out homosexuals
as worse sinners than the others mentioned. Rather than
making a special sin out of homosexuality, he simply
places it in the same category as drunkenness, theft
and fornication. In this, God demonstrates his total
impartiality toward all persons in every age. In 1
Corinthians 6:11 a pivotal statement is made: 'And
such were some of you.' Evidently, radical change has
taken place and is plain for all to see. Whether living in
circa 55 A.D. or 1994 A.D., we homosexuals who have
repented and believed the Good News have abandoned
our futile, godless way of life. What's more, the miraculous has happened: we are 'in Christ' and having
that status we are new creatures: 'the old has gone, the
new has come!' (2 Corinthians 5:17). Something of
the life of God has entered us, carrying with it far-

reaching implications, not least in how we perceive and cope with our particular sexual tendency and in how we relate to those in a similar situation.

We suggest that in all deliberations involving the homosexual question one important fact should be borne in mind: certain brothers and sisters now seeking to walk in that newness of life, and experiencing true freedom for the first time, have been rescued from backgrounds of appalling homosexual degradation and very likely premature deaths. Some of them will undoubtedly carry deep psychological scars for a long time to come. Because of that, it causes many of us profound distress and hurt to witness the extraordinary spectacle of spiritual leaders charged with feeding or ruling the flock of God apparently encouraging same-sex practices however sophisticated and refined they may appear to be. The last advice any of us redeemed homosexuals need to hear in our daily battles is that, in certain circumstances, the deeds that are 'natural' to us are permissible after all!

It must also be recognised that at the other extreme of experience, there are those—often younger Christians—who have a same-sex bias and thus far have led exemplary lives and wish to continue to do so despite pressures to the contrary. Surely any pastoral counsel given to them must be aimed at lovingly strengthening their resolve rather than undermining it by suggesting that a genital homosexual relationship can ever be God-given and God-sustained. In this delicate area, there is a real danger that 'little ones' who believe in Jesus are caused to sin.

Clearly, for all of us with homosexual leanings who follow Christ, and whatever our biographies, God has not left us to our own devices. In his love and compassion, he has freely and extravagantly given us the means to live as he intended in his flawless wisdom. He has sent the Holy Spirit to dwell in our hearts by faith bringing strength, comfort, victory, renewal and that unique fellowship for which we were created and purchased by our Lord's shed blood. Well can we gratefully say with Peter, 'his divine power has given us everything we need for life and godliness' (1 Peter 1:3).

SIX

SINGLENESS

David C Searle

For centuries, singleness in western culture was regarded as an honourable state. But with the recent dramatic rise in sexual awareness through advertising and the growth of eroticism in the media, singleness has come to be regarded as an unfulfilled condition. The result of this has been increased pressure on single young people to enter into sexual relationships; unless they do—so the hype goes—they are missing out on all the excitement and fun of life. Those involved in pastoral ministry are aware that all too often marriage has been entered into inadvisedly, sometimes because singleness has come to be regarded as highly undesirable.

The other side of the 'singleness coin' is that while the churches are making some attempt to prepare couples for marriage, and also offer counselling to those whose marriages are in difficulties, little or nothing is done to help those who are single to cope with problems they may face.

Does the Bible say anything about singleness?

Although the Bible begins with the command to the man and woman to be fruitful (have children), it is clear that certain people in the Old Testament were (honourably) unmarried. We know, for example, that Jeremiah was unmarried (Jer. 16:2), and it may well be that Elijah was also unmarried. John the Baptist was most definitely unmarried, and Paul considered singleness necessary for him to be a missionary. Philip the Evangelist had four daughters in the unmarried category who were well known for their spiritual gifts (Acts 21:8).

However, the outstanding example of a single person in the Bible is the Lord Jesus himself. No one can accuse him of leading an unfulfilled life, even though he was unmarried. Consider briefly a comment Jesus made on the unmarried state:

> For some are eunuchs because they were born that way; others were made that way by men; and others have renounced marriage because of the kingdom of heaven. The one who can accept this should accept it (Matthew 19:12).

Calvin the great reformer made this comment on Jesus's words:

> That it is not open to all to choose which state they please, Christ proves from the fact that continence [singleness] is a special gift. For when he

says that only those are capable of it to whom it is
given, he plainly means that it is not given to all.
Calvin is saying that singleness is to be regarded as a
gift of God, just as much as marriage is also a gift of
God. That is the force of Jesus' words, those to whom
it has been given. There can be little doubt this is how
we should understand what Jesus is saying.

There are three categories of single people, according to Jesus. First, there are those who were born without the physical ability to consummate a sexual marriage relationship. Second, there are those who are single through circumstances: they would like to have
been married, but the right person just never came their
way. Or perhaps for reasons outside their own control,
such as early sexual abuse or deep hurt caused by the
break-up of their own parents' marriage, these single
people have themselves never been able to face marriage. Third, there are those who have renounced marriage for the sake of the kingdom of God. Our Lord is
perhaps the best example of this third category, though
the Church's history furnishes us with countless other
examples.

The first Adam was commanded to marry and have
children. But he is not our example. The second Adam
(Christ) who is our example chose to be single so that
he could fulfil his Father's will. Perhaps that means
Christian people can make a choice because of their
Lord, and be single with highest honour in order to
serve God more effectively.

The situation Christians faced in New Testament times is very similar to the situation we face in society today. There was then and is now widespread promiscuity and sexual licence. While Paul defends the honour of marriage as divinely given to humankind, he makes it clear that sexual relationships should be confined to the marriage bond, and he also urges that singleness is a most honourable state. (See 1 Cor.7).

In the New Testament, then, single persons are welcomed as full participants in the work of the Lord. Their single status even offers pragmatic advantages for such service. But neither the single option nor a commitment to lifelong celibacy are ever set forth as the higher road to spirituality for believers.[1]

Living as a single

We have seen that Jeremiah, Elijah, John the Baptist, Paul and the daughters of Philip, as well as Jesus himself, could live fulfilled lives as single people. Ought it not, therefore, to be possible for Christians (and others) today to be happy and fulfilled as single persons? Perhaps it is time for the Church to teach again that singleness is not a condition in any way to be despised.

A choice of attitude

Those choosing to be single in order to serve God more effectively, such as ministers and missionaries who know being unmarried will give them a flexibility and freedom for service, are certainly a minority. Many others find themselves 'single by circumstance' and they have to learn to cope with a condition which is not of their choice. They have deep longings to have a sexual partner and to have children of their own. Most of all, they long to love and be loved. But the opportunity for marriage to the right person has never come their way.

The choice that single Christians must make is to reject the attitude of the world, and to adopt the attitude of Jesus Christ himself. He calls his followers to be renewed in their minds and to think as he thinks. He offers an alternative life-style which is radically different from the world's life-style. The danger for believers always is that we subconsciously adopt the world's culture and take on board the way unbelievers live. Christians who are single, therefore, must choose to think as Christ thought.

Not enough has been done, or is being done, by the churches to help single Christians to make this choice of a positive attitude towards singleness. Let me develop further what I mean.

The church family

First, single Christians do belong to a family and this needs to become more of a reality in the churches' ongoing life. It is true that some single people feel very much at home in their church fellowship; but there are many who not only do not feel at home in their churches but do not have a strong family structure to support them. Into this category come many divorcees, those with a homosexual orientation and many widow(er)s.

The Bible's theology of the Church is based on a spiritual family with God as Father, the Church as mother and Christ as our elder Brother. But few congregations make an effort to work out this theology into their ongoing programmes. The Church needs to work hard at providing the kind of family structure which will support and embrace the single people within its fellowship.

I am thinking of some very simple practical measures such as hospitality on the Lord's Day, church holidays (not necessarily formally arranged, but families within the congregation including single people in their plans). The kind of holidays which are arranged particularly for single people can actually be very unhelpful. It can be a great strain for several dozen singles to be thrown together for a week or fortnight. Many prefer to be part of a family where there are children. Few Christians ever think of inviting their single friends to share in the family experience.

Children

The mention of children leads me to a second point. Many who are single would appreciate greatly becoming close to a family with children, and being trusted to entertain the children on a regular basis to days out, or to meals or tea-parties in the single person's home. The 'aunt' or 'uncle' figure can be most important and help-ful in a child's development. But how few Christians have ever thought of adopting a single person in their fellowship to be an 'aunt' or 'uncle' to their children. At least some of those who have no children of their own would deeply appreciate the opportunity to be able to care for children at a deep level.

Sexuality does not mean sexual relationships

Third, the common misunderstanding of our society today is to confuse sexual activity and sexuality. But these two are not the same. Our sexuality is our essen-tial masculinity or femininity. Men and women were created by God to be exactly complementary. It is cer-tainly true that this complementarity is both symbol-ised and expressed within marriage by sexual union. But that is only one aspect of sexuality. Men and women can enjoy their sexuality without sexual union. They can work together and appreciate and benefit from the sexuality of the other in business or professional rela-tionships.

For sixteen years of my own ministry, I worked with a pastoral team which included both men and women. I found that I benefited immensely from the female members of the team just as much as from the male members. The women tended to think more relationally than the men. They had a particular contri-bution to make.

In such working relationships, when the sexuality

of each one finds full expression, and when that expression is appreciated and valued by the others, there will be both enjoyment and fulfilment. The work will prosper and be all the richer for such complementary relationships.

It cannot be denied that men have tended to try and dominate women, with the result that women's sexuality has been repressed and has not been allowed to have full expression. The New Testament's teaching makes it very clear that women had their proper place in the fellowship. The obvious example of this is the partnership in service of Priscilla and Aquila. Men and women have to relearn to respect the other's sexuality and to discover the enormous rewards of working together as partners. Today's feminist movement can introduce an element of rivalry which is far from the harmony there should be in Christ. Men can forestall such competitive rivalry by allowing the women's sexuality to have proper expression within the working relationships within the fellowship.

Sex

Fourth, the Bible's clear prohibition of sexual relationships outside marriage has been misrepresented in our day as narrow-mindedness which represses perfectly natural sexual desires. Why does the Bible take such a strong moral position? What is the meaning of sexual intercourse? Stanley Grenz offers a threefold explanation of sexual union within marriage.

First, the sex act recalls the commitment of husband and wife to each other. It is a kind of re-enactment of their marriage vows and is designed by God to represent and effect the marriage bonding.

Secondly, sexual intercourse is an act of mutual submission. In this way, husband and wife express to each other their desire to please each other. Sex outside a stable relationship of full commitment cannot communicate this vital element of marriage. Indeed, outwith such a stable relationship, sex will either have self-gratification as its goal or else will be a means of manipulating the other partner.

Third, sexual intercourse declares that this relationship is open to another in that procreation is effected through sex. I am not discounting the practice of family planning. But basic to sexual union is this vital possibility of bringing into being another living person in order to develop the union of husband and wife into a family. But in sex outside marriage the partners will do all possible to prevent the intrusion of a child. It follows marriage is the only proper context for sexual union.

These three meanings of sexual union ought to symbolise the life of every Church fellowship. First, the bonding of Christians within the church must be allowed often to re-enact their mutual commitment in Christ's love. Second, that bonding must be characterised by mutual submission. Thirdly, it must give birth to new life as the fellowship's evangelism brings new members into the Church's family.

Love

Fifth, single persons need just as much as married people to experience love. Note that the Bible never uses the Greek word *eros*, sexual love. Yet believers are constantly exhorted to show love, whether *agape*, *storge* or *philia*. Some fellowships are small which can make it easy for those in the 'body' to care for each other in a loving way. In larger fellowships, however, the tendency will be for people unconsciously to form unofficial groupings. That is where single people can be neglected. It doesn't take much reflection to see that being worked out in most fellowships.

I have noticed the problem especially when a single person tries to find a way into a new fellowship having moved home and job. Friendships and unofficial groups in the church are already well entrenched; single people in the church already have established friendships with other single people. So the newcomer finds him or herself at a loss to become part of the new fellowship.

How conscious is your fellowship of this problem for single people? How sensitive are you to the deep need for love in the stranger who shyly sits alone as a visitor to your church? What steps do you already take to make that person welcome and quickly become part of a loving, caring, supporting family group? The answers to these questions can at times be desolatingly disappointing!

Single people themselves can have a real sphere of service in every Christian congregation by seeking out lonely people and not only offering friendship and concern, but also going on to integrate them into the life and heart of the church. It often takes selflessness and even sacrifice for other Christians to allow the newcomers to share a place in already existing close groups of friends.

Intimacy

Sixth, as with sexuality, intimacy is often confused with sexual intercourse. So called 'one-night-stands' engage in sex without any intimacy. But many dear friends enjoy deep intimacy without ever engaging in sex. I myself have no doubt from my own pastoral experience that the single person craves more for intimacy than for a sexual relationship.

What is meant by intimacy? Intimacy requires a mutual deep personal knowledge between two people which can develop into a strong trust. Those who have such intimacy will often understand what the other person means or thinks just by a glance or picking up facial signals such as a frown or raising of the eyebrows. Those who are intimate will care for each other and will offer faithful criticism ('the wounds of a friend are faithful') as well as loving encouragement. They will share a common history and mutual memories, and will stand by each other in times of illness or difficulty.

It is sad that some who are single are afraid of this kind of deep, meaningful intimacy. It is possible that because of the deification of sex by today's society, they mistake intimacy for a sexual relationship. But David and Jonathan shared an intimate relationship without any sexual expression whatsoever (see 1 Sam. 18:1ff; 20:41f; 23:16ff; 2 Samuel 1:26).

Postscript

What about the sexual tension and frustration which many single people experience? We have to recognise that even with the love, concern, family involvement and chaste intimacy which we have outlined above, there will nevertheless still be powerful sexual desires which many find it almost impossible to cope with. Modern society with television, radio, films and magazines does much to arouse and stimulate these desires. Harold Smith makes the following comment:

> Single adults must learn to channel their sex drives
> in a way that will not offend. Thus, what one finds
> sublimating will be questionable to another. Many
> single adults find masturbation a subtle sublima-
> tion of the sex drives. It rechannels the drive from
> illicit sexual intercourse. Many singles regard mas-
> turbation as the lesser of two evils.[3]

A contrary view is given by Heather Wraight in her excellent little book in which she reminds her readers that Jesus taught the lustful look and thought was in essence as wrong as the actual deed.[4] It is vital that each person works hard at maintaining purity of mind. Every thought must be brought into captivity and be obedient to Christ. Every one of us fails many times in this way, but we must remember that there is grace to cleanse and forgive each moment of each day, and we must never abandon the fight to keep our hearts pure, as Christ is pure.

Finally, all of us need to be reminded of the dignity that Christ gave to singleness. He took little children in his arms. He shared a home and was welcomed into families such as that of Lazarus, Martha and Mary. He was especially intimate with John whom he loved. At the same time he was a man of great strength who could drive a rabble of cheating traders out of the temple court. None could deny our Lord was fulfilled, though single!

Christ himself must be the pattern for those who for whatever reason find themselves living as singles. Your attitude should be the same as that of Christ Jesus (Phil.2:5). With his help and in the bosom of his family, the church, we will find it is gloriously possible to live as he would have us live, and so to glorify his name.

SEVEN

THE MYSTERY
OF MARRIAGE

David C Searle

One of the features of American life in the minds of the British—forgive me if I am wrong—is litigation or court actions. I understand that America has more lawyers than any other of the professions, certainly far more lawyers than clergymen! I have to confess that the United Kingdom is going the same way, and people are increasingly taking court action, claiming compensation for almost anything and everything.

What the views of the Apostle Paul would be on this matter of litigation I wouldn't venture to guess. But if Paul were to take court action against all the theologians who have written about his teaching on marriage, I am quite sure he would win massive compensation for being slandered and misrepresented. What he says is infinitely more balanced and fairer to husbands and wives than many have made out. Let's look at his teaching on marriage in Ephesians 5:21ff. We will also look briefly at Peter's comments in 1 Peter 3:1-7.

Men and women equal but different

If we look at the history of the human race in general, and the history of marriage in particular, we find that men have been guilty of exploiting women. I don't think there can be any argument about that. In some civilisations, women have been regarded as the chattels of men, little better than scivvies and slaves. That is why the feminist movement has been fighting back so hard in recent years to try and recover the lost dignity of women. Do you know that even God's people, the Jews, have been guilty of this? An orthodox Jew in Jesus' day used to pray each day, 'I thank Thee God that I am neither a Gentile, a dog nor a woman.'

But what does the Bible say about men and women? We are told in Genesis 1 that God created man and woman in his own image. The man and the woman stood over against everything else that God had made, and were the very crown of God's creation. They stood side by side as equals: male and female created he them.

Their equality as persons did not mean that they were the same. The woman is called in Genesis 2 a helper suitable for the man. In case some are tempted to think the word 'helper' is rather patronising, bear in mind this word is only used 21 times in the OT, and 15 of those occurrences use it of God coming to lift up men when they have fallen and are nearly broken, and the Almighty comes to raise them up, give them fresh hope, a new start and renewed strength. So when Genesis 2 calls the woman the man's helper, it is describing her as performing a God-like task for the man. She is actually doing for the man what God also must do for him.

The word 'suitable' also needs comment. It's not easily translated from Hebrew, but it means literally one who is 'over against' or opposite to, but in the sense of being completely complementary to the man. The force of the word is that together they make the perfect couple. They are ideally matched and are made for each other.

Yet though equal in status, and perfectly complementary, they are different. They stand side by side, yes; but they also stand face to face. It is their equality in status that points to their being in God's image. But it is their difference in function that distinguishes them from God and reveals they are human, not divine. Their physical make-up tells us that.

But there is an order too, with the man created first, then the woman. The significance of that order in creation spells responsibility on the part of the man as the first-born—his it is to care and provide for the woman.

Now all this is in the thinking of Paul when he wrote about marriage as he did in Ephesians 5. Regard Genesis 1 & 2 as Act 1 in the drama of marriage and give Act 1 the title of 'Complementarity'. Ephesians 5 and I Peter 3 are in fact Act 3. Act 2 comes between Genesis 2 and Ephesians 5 and is a sorry story. That's where the exploitation begins.

Act 2 in this drama of marriage begins in Genesis 3

when sin broke into a perfect world and when a curse
came upon both the man and his wife. The wife is told
that her desire will be for her husband, but he will rule
over her. The meaning there is that she will no longer
fulfil the complementary role as she should and find
complete fulfilment in doing so, but that she will try to
dominate her husband, but he will end up dominating
her. If we were to give Act 2 a title, it would have to be
'Rivalry'. An unhappy rivalry has characterised the
sexes since the Fall, and continues to characterise the
sexes. It is not that man and woman are no longer in
essence complementary, but rather that sin has brought
in this rivalry. We see it all around us. The feminist
movement bears witness to it as women seek to challenge men's exploitation of their sex.

So what are we to call Act 3 in the Bible's drama?
Ephesians 5 describes the marriage of Christians and if
we gave this 3rd Act a title it would be 'In Christ, harmony'. Let's look then at how harmony can be achieved
by a husband and wife who are in Christ.

Mutual submission of husband and wife

'Submit to one another out of reverence for Christ'
Ephesians 5:21.

Some translations of the Bible make a paragraph divi-
sion after v21 of Ephesians 5. But rightly understood,
'submission' is always the Christian attitude in relationships. So really v21 acts as a link between what
Paul has been saying to Christians about their relation-

ships with other believers and what he is about to say to husbands and wives. In the microcosm of the family, submission is the key as it is in the macrocosm of the church.

But however can we square a mutual submission of husband and wife to each other with what Paul goes on to say about the wife's submission to her husband? The answer is not difficult to find. It is that the rôle model for both husband and wife is Christ himself.

(a) wives

> 'Wives, submit to your husbands as to the Lord. For the husband is the head of the wife as Christ is the head of the church, his body, of which he is the Saviour. Now as the church submits to Christ, so also wives should submit to their husbands in everything' Ephesians 5:22–24.

Wives are instructed to submit to their husbands because a husband is the head of the wife as Christ is the Head of the Church. Note the meaning of the word 'head'. In Hebrew thinking, the head was not thought of as the seat of the mind. The mind was identified as being in the region of the heart or chest. The head was seen rather as the source of life. That was why when someone died in Bible times, ashes were put on the head. The thought was that the spark of life had been extinguished and so ashes, the remnants of a fire that has burned itself out, were put on the head. Christ is the Head of the Church in that he is the source of the

Church's life. Our life flows from him, and only flows from him as we are joined to him as part of the Body (that is, the Church) of which he is Head. He not only sustains us, but bears responsibility for us.

In the same way, the husband is head of the wife. Headship cannot mean that the husband does all the thinking. Not at all. It is in the realm of thinking that the mutual submission comes in. What headship means is leadership, or captaincy. A captain of a team is given that rôle by the other members of the team. The captain doesn't normally seek that rôle. He is elected to it. It is the team's gift to him and it is his responsibility to lead the team. In order to be captain of his team, he must have the support of the team members. The captain may not even be the best member of the team. But as captain, he must lead.

So the wife must give her husband the captaincy of the marriage team. Unless she freely gives him that rôle, rivalry and friction will result. But why should she give him the place and responsibility of being head? Because Christ is her rôle model. He submitted to his Father. That is not to say he is not equal with the Father. Of course he is. The three Persons of the Trinity of God are co-equal. But, as Paul tells us in Philippians 5, Christ did not see equality as something to be grasped, but submitted gladly and joyfully to his Father's will and became a human being for us that he might become our Saviour. He remained equal with the Father as Son of God. But He submitted in meekness to the

77

Father's will.

Now that is how wives should submit to their husbands. Their submission to their husbands is in fact submission to the Lord. They are called on to be Christlike in the relationships with their husbands. So wives, your husbands cannot fulfil their rôle in marriage unless you help them to do so by electing them captain of your marriage team. That is the first step on the pathway to harmony in marriage.

(b) husbands

> '*Husbands, love your wives, just as Christ loved the church and gave himself up for her to make her holy, cleansing her by the washing with water through the word, and to present her to himself as a radiant church, without stain or wrinkle or any other blemish, but holy and blameless. In this same way, husbands ought to love their wives as their own bodies. He who loves his wife loves himself. After all, no-one ever hated his own body, but feeds and takes care of it, just as Christ does the church*'
> Ephesians 5:25–29.

I said a moment ago that Christ is the rôle model for both husband and wife. How is Christ the model for the husband? Paul tells us. Christ loved his bride to such an extent that he laid down his life for her and died to be her Saviour. His love was a lavish, selfless sacrificial love. That is how husbands are to love their wives, with a sacrificial, self-giving love.

Yes, husbands and wives are to share together, to
work together, to plan together. Men must listen to their
wives and must then take responsibility for decisions.
They must take action which does not consider primarily their own interests, but the interests of their wives
and children in the light of God's commands. They are
to do this because they love them.

I have been in the pastoral ministry for thirty three
years. May I tell you something? In all the marriage
counselling in which I have been engaged, I have never
once heard a wife complain that her husband loved her
too much. The interesting thing is that Paul says nothing to wives about loving their husbands. Why not? I
think the answer is easy. When a woman is truly, sacri-
ficially loved, she will respond and love in return.

So Paul sees the way to end rivalry between a husband and wife as being in the balance of wifely submission to her husband's leadership—and remember,
it is primarily a submission to the Lord Jesus—and the
husband's lavish, sacrificial love of his wife by which
he loves her and loves her and loves her.

Now husbands, how does Christ love us? Does his
love for us have any limits? Does the Lord hold your
sins and shortcomings against you? Does he reject you
because you fail him, or don't come up to standard? I
don't think so! Does Christ not love us, and forgive us,
and keep on loving us, in spite of all our shortcomings
and turning from Him? Freely, bountifully, he loves.
His love cannot be measured. It is higher, wider, deeper

than the measure of our human intellects. That is how we must love our wives. And that is the pathway to harmony in a marriage.

The glamorous wife and the considerate husband

I'm moving now from Ephesians 5 to 1 Peter 3 vs 1-7. Peter takes a very similar line to Paul in his instructions to wives and husbands, but there is a significant difference in what he says to wives. The reason for this difference is that Peter is addressing women whose husbands are not believers. These women have become Christians after their marriage, and Peter is concerned that they do their best to win their husbands for Christ. Echoing Paul, he tells them the best way to do this is by submission.

(a) the glamorous wife

'Wives, in the same way be submissive to your husbands so that, if any of them do not believe the word, they may be won over without words by the behaviour of their wives, when they see the purity and reverence of your lives. Your beauty should not come from outward adornment, such as braided hair and the wearing of gold jewellery and fine clothes. Instead, it should be that of your inner self, the unfading beauty of a gentle and quiet spirit, which is of great worth in God's sight. For this is the way the holy women of the past who put

> *their hope in God used to make themselves beau-*
> *tiful. They were submissive to their own husbands,*
> *like Sarah, who obeyed Abraham and called him*
> *her master. You are her daughters if you do what*
> *is right and do not give way to fear'* 1 Peter 3:1–
> 6.

Negatively, Peter tells wives not to preach at their husbands. A Christian wife will not normally win her husband to Christ if she lectures him. The way to win a man, says Peter, is by your behaviour. Let your life speak. He mentions three aspects of a Christian wife's life, and we will look at just one of the three: first, her purity; second, her reverence; third, her beauty. Consider the third point Peter makes, a woman's beauty.

A Christian woman, to be a good wife, must be a glamorous wife. Christian women should be stunningly beautiful. And Peter lists several ways in which this can be done. He mentions hairstyling, make-up, jewellery and clothes. But he says that in all of these a Christian wife should be extremely modest. Costly jewellery, expensive hairstyles, the latest in cosmetics and the most fashionable designer clothes are exactly what I do not mean by glamour, says Peter. What I do mean by glamour, he says, is a beautiful spirit that shines out from the heart.

I was recently in Brazil and visited some of the most deprived slum areas I have ever seen in my life. I spoke in two churches situated in these areas. I met some of the most beautiful people I have seen. Their clothes were poor and worn, yet clean and neatly mended. But the radiance, grace and glory shining from their faces was very striking. Several times as I climbed into the ramshackle car that was to take me on to my next engagement, my cheeks were wet from my tears, so moved was I after meeting and greeting these humble folk. I had seen the likeness of Jesus Christ reflected in their faces and that clear reflection brought me to tears.

Now that is the glamour Peter is speaking about. Not an outward glamour from a bottle or from expensive clothes or jewellery or coiffured hair. But an inner beauty. For the condition of our hearts will reflect itself on our faces.

Peter is not saying that Christian wives should be dowdy, and not bother with their appearance. What he is saying is that the glamour, the attractiveness that will count for Jesus Christ comes from inside us. It cannot be put on artificially.

(b) the considerate husband

> *'Husbands, in the same way be considerate as you live with your wives, and treat them with respect as the weaker partner and as heirs with you of the gracious gift of life, so that nothing will hinder your prayers'* 1 Peter 3:7.

In verse 7 of 1 Peter 3, Peter says, 'In the same way, husbands be considerate as you live with your wives, and treat them with respect as the weaker partner and as heirs with you of the grace of life.'

'In the same way', means that the principles Peter has just laid down of submission and grace apply equally to the husband. When he says, 'as heirs with you (or, together) of the grace of life', he is referring to the equality of the man and woman as standing side by side, created in God's image.

But husbands, notice that word 'considerate'. Peter is saying that husbands should always think of their wives. They should respect them, and not 'do them down'. We men can sometimes be sarcastic about our wives when we are in company. I know there is a jocular way of speaking and I am sometimes guilty of that. But it is easy to show lack of respect for our wives and so to show lack of loving consideration for them.

Two reasons are given why we men must be considerate in this tender, loving way. The first is that the woman is different to the man. Physically, emotionally and relationally, she is different. Recognise those differences, respect and honour those differences. A wife needs special consideration because hers is the role of bearing children, caring for them and nurturing them in their early years. I know husbands have a share in that task, but the wife has a deeper, more internal way of relating to her children. She needs her husband, but she needs him to be particularly considerate to her in all she is called on to do and be as a woman.

The second reason given for special consideration is that husband and wife stand together, side by side, in the presence of God, cleansed by Christ, loved and redeemed by him, made members together of his Father's family, and accepted by grace that is boundless and free. While physically and emotionally she is different, she is nonetheless a joint heir with her husband of the grace of life.

Now can we gather all this together? How are we getting along in our marriages? What I mean is, how do our marriages compare with God's pattern for husbands and wives? Follow through for just a moment Act 1, 2 and 3. Act 1: Complementarity. I hope it's not too silly to ask if we have grasped that complementary nature of our relationship, that men and women are equal in status, but different in function. There is a great deal of modern rubbish talked about this, you know. Feminism recognises the equality, but tends to lose sight of the difference. Men and women are not the same. If we were the same, then gay and lesbian relationships would be alright. But we are different in a fundamental and vital way which makes a man and woman exactly complementary to each other in a way which homosexual relationships lack—they do not have that complementary difference and that is why they are flawed and wrong. A man and woman need each other, and make together the perfect pair; two halves of the apple! So, have we recognised the wonder of Act 1?

Act 2: Rivalry. It may be that present today is one

ideal couple in 100,000! I very occasionally have met
couples who told me they had never had a cross word
in forty years of marriage. Well, I have to admit that
my wife and I can't say that. Most of us have experi-
enced that uneasy rivalry which comes as a result of
the Fall. A tension as the wife tries to persuade her
husband to listen to her and the husband is foolishly
determined to do his own thing and ignore his wife's
interests and wishes.

Many marriages have a dark shadow over them,
and only rarely does the sun shine on them from a
cloudless sky. Any shaky marriages today? With
grudges being harboured, and communication break-
ing down? Tensions which will not go away, but which
are fed by attitudes and prejudices which lack both
understanding and submission?

Maybe the rivalry arises from stolen love. Your love
has been given to another, and is not wholly given to
your wife or husband. And so rivalry and tension is
sharp, even bitter. Act 2 is being played out in your life
and the consequences are unhappiness for you and in-
security for your children. Is it time to close the curtain
on Act 2 and usher in Act 3: In Christ, Harmony?

Harmony, as both husband and wife make Christ
himself their rôle model. Mutual submission, with the
wife giving her husband as her special wedding gift
the place of head, and the husband lavishing his wife
with sacrificial love. Harmony because the wife's concern is inner beauty, the beauty of a godly life, and the

husband's concern is to be considerate and give his wife the utmost respect and honour.

So, how is Act 3 going? I have my wife's permission to say this: we met when we were seventeen, and dated each other for six years before we married at age 23. We soon discovered that we were possibly the most incompatible pair that ever married. So our marriage has not been easy. Most of the fault has been on my side. But over the years, I have been learning some insights into the mystery of how marriage can work and be harmonious. Those insights come from God's Word. And I believe I can say that today we must be among the happiest married couples living in Edinburgh. After 36 years, we are deeply in love, more deeply in love than ever, and harmony is the keynote of our lives. Not that it is always easy, but that it is gloriously possible, and we prove it every day.

So how about you? Take the Word of God seriously. Wives, dare to submit to your husbands, as you submit to the Lord. Husbands, guard your hearts and save your love exclusively for your wives and just heap that love on them, not in ostentatious ways, but from deep within. Love them and love them and love them! Remember that love is not foremost an emotion, but an act of the will, an act of obedience to Christ. We love, because he first loved us.

EIGHT

EPILOGUE

David C Searle

Is there any response that the churches should be making today to the massive assault which is being brought against the traditional biblical standards of morality? Ought those of us who profess to be Christians to be taking any clear action to stem the floodtide of increasing sexual chaos? Are the Bible's standards still relevant today? And as we move into the twenty-first century, is Christianity still a force to be reckoned with?

There are several ways in which the Christian church can react to the sexual revolution which is going on all around us. One would be to allow our standards slowly and imperceptibly to be eroded as the shadow of the world's hand moves silently over the church's life. It cannot be denied that to some extent that is already happening. There are congregations where immorality is openly tolerated among elders. There are fellowships in which extra-marital relationships are by no means a closely guarded secret. And there is an unnoticed change in moral attitudes among many who claim to be followers of Jesus Christ. The constant, inexora-

ble deluge of media propaganda is relentlessly taking
its toll of many believers' attitudes.

This erosion of biblical morality within the churches
requires to be recognised for what it is—a threat ulti-
mately to the church's very existence (see Rev.3:20-
23).

Another possible response by the church is to act as
if nothing needs to be done and no changes are necessary. Many express the opinion that in time the tide
will turn and there will be a swing back to more traditional attitudes. There are many sincere believers who
voice this pious, but improbable, hope. The ostrich likewise hopes danger will disappear if it hides its head in
the sands!

No. The church must change. Christians must adopt
a clear, deliberate strategy to defend the validity and
truth of the Bible's teaching on morality and they must
also actively promote the values which are offered to
us in Christ. I make the following suggestions which
may appear deceptively simple but which I believe
could have profound effects for good.

First, biblical teaching on morality should be ex-
plicitly taught from our pulpits, in our Bible Classes
and for every age and stage of the Christian family. It is
no use hoping that young people will somehow 'pick
up' the Scripture's reasoning and values. The propaganda from society and the media is powerful, constant, explicit and compelling, appealing as it does to
fallen human nature. It can only be countered by firm,

clear teaching which cannot be misunderstood.

I am not suggesting the old moralistic ranting about immorality be revived in the pulpits of the land, but rather that 'bridges' be built from the 'then and there' of Scripture to the 'here and now' of contemporary society. In other words, the problems need to spelt out. The provision of God for our good needs to be lovingly shown. The consequences of disobedience need to be explained. All this, without embarrassment but chastely taught in a relevant, realistic way.

There is a note to be sounded which is seldom heard. It is that close friendship need not have a sexual orientation. It is increasingly assumed by our generation that where there is friendship, there must inevitably be a sexual undertone. C.S.Lewis deplored this attitude in his book *The Four Loves*. But his warning appears to have gone unnoticed and unheeded. The churches need to recover the concept and reality of wholesome friendship as exemplified in the relationship between David and Jonathan. I know that today aspersions are cast that theirs must have been a homosexual love. But in Israel such practices were abhorred, while chaste friendship was exalted. The churches must eloquently and persistently affirm the honour of the chaste friendship between Christians of the same sex.

That such teaching is not being given at present is self-evident. This is the first response that is urgently called for. Hence this book.

Second, the family needs to be powerfully affirmed

on two distinct levels. There is the microcosm of the nuclear family. There is also the macrocosm of the church family. Unwittingly, the church herself has been the agent of disintegration of the family at both levels. Much church life divides members of the fellowship on the grounds of both age and gender. The accommodation the churches provide is often designed exactly for this purpose—to separate the members off into various little groups. But the church should be a great uniting agent bringing her members together in a manner that spans all barriers of age and gender, not least in her services of worship on the Lord's Day.

Those who have the oversight of Christian congregations of all denominations ought to be working hard at promoting family values for each home and for the wider fellowship.

Third, each church should also be working hard to provide pastoral care for those who are in special need of moral help. Too often, when a brother or sister makes a moral slip, the response is one of condemnation and isolation. Too often, there is a lack of understanding, compassion and ongoing support, especially for those who repeatedly fall.

In this regard, few congregations (or groups of congregations) make any provision for those who, through no fault of their own, find their sexual orientation is not 'straight'. Many a homosexual has suffered for years in silence, enduring unthinkable agonies and frustration, longing for someone with whom to share their secret and who will offer loving friendship and patient support.

I am convinced it ought to be openly known that within each area of Christian churches there is the equivalent of a 'help-line' for homosexuals who are struggling with their awful burden. It would be in the hands of some person(s), suitably trained and spiritually mature, set apart by the church for this ministry, and whose confidentiality is assured. Weekly intimation sheets which many congregations now have should give such a 'help-line' telephone number.

Some smaller congregations may not be able to resource this kind of provision. But groups of congregations working together should be able to work out a practicable scheme and so offer help to those who without such support may well be enticed by the treacherous seductions of a godless society and find warmer friendship and understanding in a gay pub or club.

§

In all of this, our great Exemplar is Christ himself. The church is his Body. Too seldom the local community sees the radiant face of Christ, or hears his gracious voice, or experiences the warmth of His love. We will only be true to our holy calling when Christ is not only among us, but when we as the family of God become very Christ to our communities. And that can only be when holiness, compassion and love emanate from our common life together. May God grant that this will be increasingly so for his glory.

Notes on ch 2

1   John Boswell, *Christianity, Social Tolerance, and Homosexuality*, Chicago 1980

2   Robin Scroggs, *The New Testament and Homosexuality*, Philadelphia 1983

3   L. William Countryman, *Dirt, Greed and Sex*, London 1989

4   Richard B. Hays, 'Relations, Natural and Unnatural: A Response to John Boswell's Exegesis of Romans 1' in *The Journal of Religious Ethics*, 14 (1986) pp. 184–215

5   David F. Wright, 'Homosexuality: The Relevance of the Bible' in *The Evangelical Quarterly* 61:6 (1989), pp. 291–300

6   Thomas E. Schmidt, *Impurity and Sin in Romans 1.26–27* (an unpublished paper—a response to Countryman). See now his treatment in *Straight and Narrow? Compassion and Clarity in the Homosexuality Debate*, Leicester, IVP, 1995.

7   *Op. cit.,* p. 1

8   *Op. cit.,* p. 1

9   J. C. Beker, 'The Faithfulness of God and the Priority of Israel in Paul's Letter to the Romans' in K P Donfried (ed.) *The Romans Debate*, Peabody, Mass. 1991, pp. 329–332

10 F. F. Bruce, writing on Romans 1.18 in *The Epistle to the Romans*, London, 1963, *ad loc.*

11 *Op. cit.,* pp. 4–18

12 Both quotations from C. E. B. Cranfield, *Romans: A Shorter Commentary*, Edinburgh 1985, *ad loc.*
13 D. F. Wright, *op. cit.,* p. 295
14 *Op. cit.,* p. 206
15 George R. Edwards, *Gay/Lesbian Liberation: A Biblical Perspective*, New York 1984
16 *Op. cit.,* p. 209

Notes on ch 4

1 Liz Hodgkinson, 'Body and Mind: Lightness of Being Celibate' in *The Times.* Tuesday 19th January 1993
2 *Submission on Human Sexuality*, Forum Paper published by Rutherford House, 1993

Notes on ch 6

1 Stanley Grenz, *Sexual Ethics*, Word Publishing, Dallas, 1990, p.167
2 Stanley Grenz, *ibid.*, pp.181-2
3 Eph. 5:21
4 *agape* means 'self-giving love', *storge* means 'friendship', *philia* means 'family love'
5 Harold Ivan Smith, *Single and Feeling Good*, Abingdon Press, Nashville, 1987, p.54
6 Heather Wraight, *Single the Jesus Model*, Crossway Books, Leicester, 1995, p.83